Wild Anim

RED FOXES

GAIL TERP

BLACK
RABBIT
BOOKS

Bolt is published by Black Rabbit Books
P.O. Box 3263, Mankato, Minnesota, 56002.
www.blackrabbitbooks.com
Copyright © 2017 Black Rabbit Books

Design and Production by Michael Sellner
Photo Research by Rhonda Milbrett

Library of Congress Control Number: 2015954913

HC ISBN: 978-1-68072-057-0   PB ISBN: 978-1-68072-314-4

Printed in the United States at CG Book Printers,
North Mankato, Minnesota, 56003. 8/17

Web addresses included in this book were working and appropriate
at the time of publication. The publisher is not responsible for
broken or changed links.

Image Credits

Corbis: F. Lukasseck/Masterfile, 23;
Jeremy Woodhouse/Blend Images, 24 (bottom); Reinhard Hölzl/imageBROKER, 25 (top
left); Robert Postma/First Light, 25 (top right); Steve
Kaufman, 24 (top); Yva Momatiuk & John Eastcott/Min-
den Pictures, 26 (bottom); Marcus Siebert, 11; Dreamstime:
Isselee, 31; Getty: Colin Carter Photography, Cover; iStock:
Anagramm, 8–9; janeff, 3; Piotr Krze lak, 25 (bottom); rytters-
foto, Back Cover, 1, 12; National Geographic Creative: ALASKA
STOCK IMAGES, 20; BARRETT HEDGES, 6–7; Shutterstock:
alslutsky, 29 (dragonfly); ArtHeart, 16–17; BERNATSKAYA OXA-
NA, 29 (ant); Debbie Steinhausser, 15; DragoNika, 32; Eric Isselee, 14, 29 (bear & mouse); FloridaStock, 29 (eagle); francesco de
marco, 19; Giedriius, 26 (top); HHelene, 29 (beetle); lantapix,
16–17 (background); merkulovstudio, 29 (fox); Preto Perola,
29 (berries); r.classen, 29 (fly); robert_s, 13 (left); sivivolk,
13 (right); Thomas Zsebok, 4–5; Ultrashock, 29 (wolf)
Every effort has been made to contact copyright
holders for material reproduced in this book.
Any omissions will be rectified in subse-
quent printings if notice is given
to the publisher.

Contents

CHAPTER 1

A Day in the

It's late evening. A red fox leaves its **den** to hunt. It trots along, sniffing as it goes. When it smells food, it stops to dig. There are three turtle eggs. It eats them in three gulps.

The fox moves on. At a field, it stops to listen. A faint rustle comes from the grass.

Catch!

One of the fox's large ears turns toward the sound. This turning helps the fox know where **prey** is hiding. The fox walks slowly toward the sound.

Close to the sound, the fox stops.
It raises its front legs off the ground
and jumps up. It pounces on a mouse.
With one swallow, the mouse is gone.

RED FOX FEATURES

WHITE-TIPPED FLUFFY TAIL

WHITE BELLY

REDDISH-BROWN FUR

EARS

POINTED MUZZLE

BLACK LEGS AND FEET

9

CHAPTER 2

Food to Eat

and a Place to Live

Red foxes are **omnivores**. They mostly eat small prey, such as mice and rabbits. They also eat insects and worms. For plants, they eat grass, fruit, and nuts. Given the chance, they eat garbage too.

Hunting

A red fox hunts alone. It pounces on mice and bites at insects. For larger prey, such as rabbits, it sneaks up as close as it can. Then it runs at its prey and grabs it with its teeth.

Worm Hunting

An earthworm is a treat for a red fox. It grabs the worm's head with its teeth. The worm slides out of the soil and slips down the fox's throat.

Home Sweet Home

Red foxes are found throughout the northern part of the world. They live in fields and on the edges of woods. Some live in deserts. They are found on farms and in towns too. Most red foxes live in dens in the ground.

How Big Is a Red Fox? · · · · ·

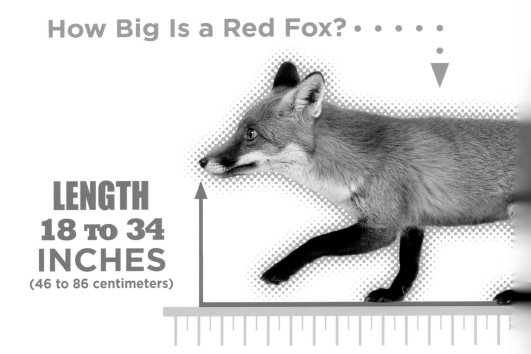

LENGTH
18 TO 34
INCHES
(46 to 86 centimeters)

WEIGHT

6.5 TO 24 POUNDS
(3 to 11 kilograms)

0 pounds — 5 — 10 — 15 — 20 25 30 — 35 — 40 — 45 — 50 pounds

WHERE RED FOXES LIVE

Red Fox Range Map

Male and female fox pairs stay together for life. They may dig their own dens. Or they might use dens left by other animals. Red fox pairs will often use the same dens for years.

COMPARING SIZES

pup
about .2 POUND
(91 grams)

adult
about 15 POUNDS
(6,804 grams)

pounds 0   2

20

Time for Pups

Red fox pups are born in the spring. They spend the first few weeks in their dens. They drink milk from their mothers. After five weeks, they come out of the dens. They eat the food their parents bring until they are four months old.

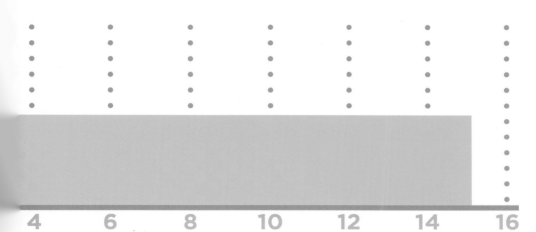

4   6   8   10   12   14   16

Pup Hunters

In summer, the pups go with their parents to hunt. By the end of summer, they can hunt for themselves. In the fall, most pups leave to start their own families.

The first few weeks in a den are peaceful. But then the pups start to fight over food. The best fighters get the most to eat.

By the Numbers

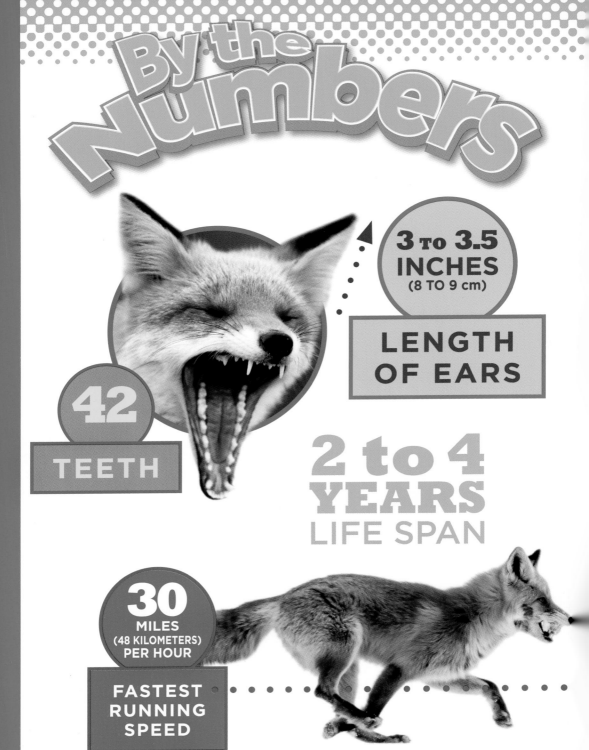

3 TO 3.5 INCHES (8 TO 9 cm)
LENGTH OF EARS

42 TEETH

2 to 4 YEARS LIFE SPAN

30 MILES (48 KILOMETERS) PER HOUR
FASTEST RUNNING SPEED

2 TO 12
AVERAGE NUMBER OF PUPS BORN AT ONE TIME

1.1 TO 2.2 POUNDS
(0.5 TO 1 kg)

FOOD EATEN PER DAY

6.5 TO 7 FEET
(2 TO 2.1 METERS)

JUMPING HEIGHT

In the Garden

Red foxes can help gardeners. Rabbits eat lots of crops. Red foxes eat many of the rabbits.

CHAPTER 4

Predators
and Other Threats

Red fox adults have few **predators**. But their pups have many. Eagles, bears, and wolves hunt pups. To keep pups safe, parents watch them closely.

Humans are the greatest threat to red foxes. They build on the land where foxes live. They hunt and trap them. Farmers kill red foxes to protect their livestock.

Red Fox Ecosystem

Red foxes are good for their **ecosystems**. They eat mice and rats, keeping them out of cities and farms. Their **scat** also spreads the seeds of fruit they eat. Red foxes are an important part of the animal kingdom.

Red Fox Food Chain

This **food chain** shows what eats red foxes. It also shows what red foxes eat.

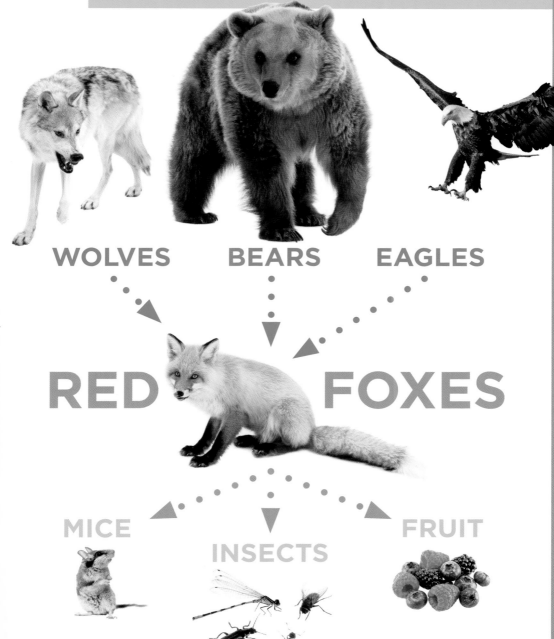

WOLVES   BEARS   EAGLES

RED FOXES

MICE
INSECTS
FRUIT

den (DEN)—the home of some kinds of wild animals

ecosystem (E-co-sys-tum)—a community of living things in one place

food chain (FOOD CHAYN)—a series of plants and animals in which each uses the next in the series as a food source

omnivore (AHM-ni-vor)—an animal that eats both plants and animals

predator (PRED-uh-tuhr)—an animal that eats other animals

prey (PRAY)—an animal hunted or killed for food

scat (SKAT)—the waste, or poop, left by an animal

BOOKS

Arnosky, Jim. *Wild Tracks: A Guide to Nature's Footprints.* New York: Sterling Pub. Co., 2015.

Borgert-Spaniol, Megan. *Red Foxes.* North American Animals. Minneapolis: Bellwether Media, Inc., 2015.

Strother, Ruth. *Red Foxes.* Wild Canine Pups. New York: Bearport Pub., 2014.

WEBSITES

Red Fox
animals.nationalgeographic.com/animals/ mammals/red-fox/

Red Fox
www.biokids.umich.edu/critters/Vulpes_vulpes/

Red Fox
www.dkfindout.com/us/animals-and-nature/dogs/ red-fox/